PORTAL

MICHAEL JEFFERSON

Copyright © 2021 Michael Jefferson
All rights reserved
First Edition

Fulton Books, Inc.
Meadville, PA

Published by Fulton Books 2021

ISBN 978-1-63860-574-4 (paperback)
ISBN 978-1-63860-575-1 (digital)

Printed in the United States of America

2 YEARS

I thought I heard your voice again today.
I thought I saw your face in the crowd yesterday.
You are in every song. You are in every show.
You are everywhere I go. You are in everything I do.
There is always something that reminds me of you.
I feel you in the air. I turn around, but you are not there.
If this is magic, how do I make this pain disappear?

*Baby, it has been two years since you have been gone.
Two years is much too long. In two years, I have cried so many tears.
Although you're gone, the pain is still here.
Your memory will never disappear.*

I see your face in my head, but I still sleep alone in this bed.
I think of you with every breath. How do
I stop this pain? I had enough.

*Baby, it has been two years since you have been gone.
Two years is much too long. In two years, I have cried so many tears.
Although your gone, the pain is still here.
Your memory will never disappear.*

I still can't believe that you are gone.
Everyone tells me life goes on.
I continue this journey down the road.
With a heavy heart, I walk alone.
One day, my journey will end and a new one begins.
When we are together in heaven again.

*Baby, it has been two years since you have been gone.
Two years is much too long. In two years, I have cried so many tears.
Although your gone, the pain is still here.
Your memory will never disappear.*

July 5, 2018

ABUSE

He tells her that she is special. Something she never knew.
He wants her to be his one and only. She
is just tired of being lonely.
He promises her the world, if she will be his girl.
The world is their oyster, and she is the pearl.
She is full of hopes and dreams.
They are trapped inside her, and she wants to scream.
She just wants a change, but she cannot break free from her chains.
He promises to break her chains; she just got to take his name.
He sets her free and seals the deal with a diamond ring.

*We know the story all too well. Girl falls for boy.
Paradise turns to hell. He once told you you're a
special chick, but now he just calls you bitch.*

She finds out quick love is not what it seems.
She is barely holding onto her dreams.
She has to finish dinner before he gets home;
if not, the beast breaks another bone.
He said he had a bad day—fetch him a rum and coke.
Please do not spill it so you do not get choked.
Slaving all day for a slap in the face. Something
must have been out of place.
Hopefully the kids do not make a sound. You do
not know if you can survive another round.
The prince you first met is now a beast. He
has you and your children on a leash.
What can you do? Where can you go? How
do you escape this beast's control?
This man once promised to be your savior; now he is your slaver.
Think of your children. Think of yourself. Do
what you must to be somewhere else.
The time has come for you to be brave.
If you don't, you will be staring at a grave.

*We know the story all too well. Girl falls for boy.
Paradise turns to hell. He once told you you're a
special chick, but now he just calls you bitch.*

June 24, 2017

ALCOHOL LOVE

In the morning, when I awoke, I thought to myself, *Is this a joke?*
My beauty queen went from a 10 to a 2.
Oh man, what did I do?

Alcohol love, what did you do with the girl that I met last night?
She looked so fine. Everything just right.
Alcohol love, what did you do to my eyes?
Oh man, she had a great disguise.

When I looked you in the eye, I knew it was time for goodbye.
You thought it was love. You thought it would last.
Get over it, girl. It is in the past.
I told you goodbye and tried to leave. You
got mad and started to scream.
This is a nightmare, far from a dream.
You call me a liar. You call me a fake.
There was no spark. There was no fire. Please
stop yelling. I got a headache.

Alcohol love, what did you do with the girl that I met last night?
She looked so fine. Everything just right.
Alcohol love, what did you do to my eyes?
Oh man, she had a great disguise.

I tried to tell you this is a onetime thing.
Now you expect a diamond ring.
I gather my stuff off the floor. You tell me to use the backdoor.
I head for home, but I stop for a drink. I sit there and start to think.
This is how I got here. Screw it; give me a beer.

November 14, 2017

BIG-CITY DREAMS

She was a lonely girl in a lonely town.
Saturday nights always bring her down.
Big lights of the city calling her name.
Going to go searching for fortune and fame.
She had the perfect family, but she had stars in her eyes.
To blind to see. She got to follow her dreams.

Big-city dreams—selling lies on the silver screen.
Big-city dreams—grass isn't always greener on the other side.
Don't need a ticket for this ride.
Big-city dreams—never felt so all alone. What the hell am I doing here?
I just want to go home.

She left a note for mom and dad. "I'm going to
be on the silver screen. Don't be sad."
She met a man. He told her he had a plan.
Going to take her to the top, can't you hear the champagne pop?
You're going to be the next Marilyn Monroe;
all you got to do is sell your soul.

Big-city dreams—selling lies on the silver screen.
Big-city dreams—grass isn't always greener on the other side.
Don't need a ticket for this ride.
Big-city dreams—never felt so all alone. What the hell am I doing here?
I just want to go home.

All the glamour and limousines. All the fame and magazines.
Promises so hard to find. Tell me is it worth
the broken hearts you left behind.

Big-city dreams—selling lies on the silver screen.
Big-city dreams—grass isn't always greener on the other side.
Don't need a ticket for this ride.
Big-city dreams—never felt so all alone. What the hell am I doing here?
I just want to go home.

March 27, 1990

Broken Heart

You are everywhere, but nowhere. In my head, your voice I hear.
I open my eyes to my worst fear. I reach out
to touch you, and you are not there.

Everywhere I go, I see you. The heart sees what it wants to see.
Everywhere I go, I feel you. The heart feels what it wants to feel.
I know my love for you is real. Now you are gone, and I miss you.
I shed a tear; what else can I do?
Everyone tells me that they understand. But
do they know my pain is real?
Tell me if you truly understand, how long
does it take a broken heart to heal?

Thinking of you always brings a smile, but it never lasts too long.
It gets replaced by heartache and sorrow. Push
it away and deal with it tomorrow.

Everywhere I go, I see you. The heart sees what it wants to see.
Everywhere I go, I feel you. The heart feels what it wants to feel.
I know my love for you is real. Now you are gone, and I miss you.
I shed a tear what else can I do?
Everyone tells me that they understand. But
do they know my pain is real?
Tell me if you truly understand, how long
does it take a broken heart to heal?

They say time heals all wounds. Well, I guess
there is nothing left for me to do.
I sit here, going insane. Waiting for time to erase my pain.

Everywhere I go, I see you. The heart sees what it wants to see.
Everywhere I go, I feel you. The heart feels what it wants to feel.
I know my love for you is real. Now you are gone, and I miss you.
I shed a tear what else can I do?

*Everyone tells me that they understand. But
do they know my pain is real?
Tell me if you truly understand, how long
does it take a broken heart to heal?*

November 7, 2017

CHOICES

Choices begin when you are small.
Did you choose to color on the wall?
It is like studying for a test and hoping your choice is the best.
Some choices are made with the heart.
Some are made without all the facts.
Some choices are made with the mind.
Some are too damn hard to find.

Choices are made every day. They affect our lives in every way.
Some choose to live, and some live in fear.
Some bring a smile, and some bring a tear.
Whether or not you choose to choose is up to you.
But be warned, some choices are made for you.

Do you choose to lead, or do you follow the crowd?
Do you choose to fly with your dreams, or
are your feet planted on the ground?
Do you choose to listen when they call you names?
Do you choose to play their games?
Do you choose to fight, or do you have the strength to walk away?
Did you choose to take those drugs?
Did you choose to wear that glove?
Say goodbye to the freedoms you had.
Do you choose to be a man, to be a dad?

Choices are made every day. They affect our lives in every way.
Some choose to live, and some live in fear.
Some bring a smile, and some bring a tear.
Whether or not you choose to choose is up to you.
But be warned, some choices are made for you.

Did you choose to kiss that girl?
Did you choose to make her your world?
Did you choose to love her until you die?
Did you choose to make her your bride?
If she gets sick, will you choose to stay?
How can you walk away?

Choices are made every day. They affect our lives in every way.
Some choose to live, and some live in fear.
Some bring a smile, and some bring a tear.
Whether or not you choose to choose is up to you.
But be warned, some choices are made for you.

Did you choose to laugh when you wanted to cry?
Did you choose to pray to God for a little more time?
Did you choose to confess your love?
Did you choose to let her go and fly above?
Did you choose bended knee and hands clasped while
your one and only slips through your grasp?

Choices are made every day. They affect our lives in every way.
Some choose to live, and some live in fear.
Some bring a smile, and some bring a tear.
Whether or not you choose to choose is up to you.
But be warned, some choices are made for you.

July 11, 2018

CORRUPTER OF SOULS

Drugs are a deadly game. They do not
discriminate and have no shame.
They lead to death and corruption of your
soul. Can you feel the anxiety grow?
You need another hit, another fix. Can you
see your body lying in a ditch?
He has many allies to pull you in. Fill you
with temptation. You know it is a sin.
He takes the form of darkness that will lead to death.
In your darkest hour, he will take your last breath.
He will lie to you. He tells you he is your friend,
but it will only lead to your end.
If you think it is bad, it will only get worse.
Can you see the people following the hearse? Can
you see the people crying over a grave?
Tell me, do you still think you will be saved?

The corrupter of souls lives inside of you.
He controls how you think. He controls what you do.
He fills your mind and heart with hate.
What are you going to do now? It is too late.

You cry out for mercy, but you will find none.
You think the solution is in the drug.
A final plea for your life. The corrupter of souls laughs in the night.
You pull up your sleeve. You tie the knot.
Everything will be better with this shot.
You extend the arm. You cannot see the harm.
Russian roulette without the gun. The
corrupter of souls' work is done.

The corrupter of souls lives inside of you.
He controls how you think. He controls what you do.
He fills your mind and heart with hate.
What are you going to do now? It is too late.

You have lost this deadly game. The
corrupter of souls' army still gains.
You had your chance as you slip into the numb.
Now your dance with death has begun.

September 30, 2012

Dark Ages

The king has ruled fair and right. He has
ruled with all his wisdom and might.
The time for decision will come tonight.
We have tried, but we cannot take it
anymore. Now it is time for war.
We assemble our bravest knights. The captain of
the guard says, "Finally, the time is right."
The mystic advises the king that when the sun aligns
with the moon, the battle will commence very soon.
We have fought many foes and turned many men into ghost. We
fought armies twice our size. We spit into the dragon's eyes.
We have fought many wizards with evil spells
and have sent demons back to hell.
Through the years, we have fought and prospered very well.

This is the time of the dark ages. This is the time to be
strong, for the weak will crumble to the ground.
This is the time of the dark ages. This is the time to be
brave. Defeat evil, and our kingdom we will save.

Our king leads us to battle. We fight so hard and strike so fast.
Their soldiers tremble at our feet. There is
no retreat. Their army lies beat.
All we know is fight. Fight for the weak. Fight for our king.
Fight for everything that we hold dear and never show fear.

This is the time of the dark ages. The sword rules the land.
This is the time of the dark ages. Evil was
defeated, and the party would be grand.

April 25, 1989

Dark Knight

It's a rainy night in the city.
We can't find a ride—what a pity.
The show is over, and it is time to go home.
We decided to walk, but we are not alone.
Bullets scream out into the silence.
This morning I heard the mayor talking about the violence.
Oh god! Why is this happening to me?
They say mom and dad are gone, but I refuse to believe.
I fall down on my knees.
Please. Please, let's turn back the clock.
I still feel the ringing in my ears from the shots.
Someone has got to make it stop.

It's a dark knight in the city.
What happened to this place?
It's a dark knight in the city.
Will we ever feel safe?
Everybody is scared. Who is going to take away the fear?
Stay out of the shadows.
They are creeping up on you.
You never know who is watching you.

Fueled by anger. Driven by hate.
I should have done something, but now it is too late.
The cops have no clues to solve this riddle.
Why do I feel like I'm stuck in the middle?
The cops asked me what I saw.
I tried to remember, but my memory was flawed.
There was a cat that caught my attention.
She made me look in the other direction.
I heard a loud noise, and I saw a gun.
Down the alley, I saw a man run.
I try to swallow my fears.
I wipe away my tears.

Inside I'm screaming, but no one hears.
Full of anxiety, it makes me choke.
I hear laughing in the shadows, but it is no joke.

It's a dark knight in the city.
What happened to this place?
It's a dark knight in the city.
Will we ever feel safe?
Everybody is scared. Who is going to take away the fear?
Stay out of the shadows.
They are creeping up on you.
You never know who is watching you.

I sneak into the shadows to see what I can find.
It is like living in a nightmare with this fear injected into my mind.
I hear a voice, and it scares me to death.
Please, God, don't let that be my last breath.
Watch out for that poison ivy.
It will make you itch.
Stay away! She is a nasty bitch.
Little boy, stop!
Turn and run away, or you will end up being
food in the sewer for the killer croc.

April 18, 2021

Death of the Mother

Live for today and not tomorrow.
Do what you will and feel no sorrow.
Does anybody really care? Denounce your mother, if you dare.
Don't care about the future; don't care what you do. Poison the water and the air too.
You will live forever; you think you are so cool.
Breaking the rules, now you play the fool.
A slap in the face. A stab in the back.
Keep on running and never look back.
Our future looks so grim as mother's light dims.

The earth dies screaming—does anybody care?
No, you are not dreaming; the earth dies screaming.

Pollution takes away her breath.
Ignorance leads to our death.
Life of a million years slip through our fingers and disappear.
Money's all that we desire. It only took a spark to start the fire.
Sit back and watch the flames grow high.
Now we watch Mother burn. Get in line; soon it will be your turn.
Can you see the crack in the sky?
Can you not hear Mother's cry?

The earth dies screaming—does anybody care?
No, you are not dreaming; the earth dies screaming.

As we snuff out Mother's candle of life.
She can no longer fight.
Death is at our door, and an egotistical human race laughs no more.

The earth dies screaming—does anybody care?
No, you are not dreaming; the earth dies screaming.

June 15, 1989

DREAMS

You work hard every day, but nobody cares.
There got to be a better way, but you have
not found your way there.
This is a journey; you got to go it alone.
No one said it was easy. You got a bumpy road.
You say your prayers before you go to sleep; maybe
in the morning, your dreams you can keep.

Follow your dreams. It is a dream come true.
Follow your dreams. It was meant for you.
Follow your dreams. Do not let them take it away.
Follow your dreams. You got to fight every day.

Plenty of people put you down. They say you
cannot make it; you are just a clown.
They are just full of insecurities. They cling
on you like some damn disease.
Full of jealousy and hate. They try to
change your mind and your fate.

Follow your dreams. It is a dream come true.
Follow your dreams. It was meant for you.
Follow your dreams. Do not let them take it away.
Follow your dreams. You got to fight every day.

It is hard to count the tears that you cried. Do
not let them put out your fire inside.

Follow your heart. You got to keep the faith.
When you get lost it will show you the way.
Follow your dreams—may they all come true.
Follow your dreams and believe in you.

January 25, 2017

Empty Words

From the start, it was a lie. You broke my heart; our love just died.
You say you love me and that is a fact, but
here we are, and it is the final act.
You pull me close and say do not let go.
There is no encore to this show.
You hurt me with your lies; all I got is tears and pain inside.
I cannot believe I fell for your lies.

Empty words are all you say, every night every day.
Empty words have no meaning, and as time goes by, even less feeling.
I want you to know that this is no joke; on
your empty words, I hope you choke.

You were great. You played your part. Like
a hunter, you trapped my heart.
I was the trusting fool. I cannot believe I fell for you.
You like to manipulate everyone just to get your way.
You are the star in your own play.

Empty words are all you say, every night every day.
Empty words have no meaning, and as time goes by, even less feeling.
I want you to know that this is no joke; on
your empty words, I hope you choke.

You say that you are full of fear; is that a
smile I see through your tears?
You beg me not to go. The curtains are
falling; it is the end of the show.
No Oscar or Golden Globe; you think you played the perfect role.

Empty words are all you say, every night every day.
Empty words have no meaning, and as time goes by, even less feeling.
I want you to know that this is no joke; on
your empty words, I hope you choke.

FATHER

Dedicated to David Patistea

You taught me more than you know.
It is not always a weakness to let your emotions show.
When life is hectic, you got to take it slow.
Sometimes, that is just how life goes.
You taught me not to hug a man but look
him in the eyes and shake his hand.
Respect is not bought but earned.
Thank you, Dad, for another lesson learned.

*Father, you showed me you don't always have to use
your hands to prove that you are a man.
Sometimes, you got to turn the cheek, and
sometimes you got to make a stand.
Father, thank you for making me the man that I am.
Father, you taught me always to protect your family.
Thank you, Father, for believing in me.
Thank you for being you.
Father, I love you.*

Remember when you taught me to ride a bike?
It was much more than that.
When you fall it will hurt, but you get back up.
You bought me my first glove. Not to fear
life because life could be fun.
Remember when you taught me to drive?
It was a gas. Even when the trooper made us take
down the flag. The three-point turn almost did me in,
but you were there to pull me through again.

*Father, you showed me you don't always have to use
your hands to prove that you are a man.
Sometimes you got to turn the cheek, and
sometimes you got to make a stand.
Father, thank you for making me the man that I am.
Father, you taught me always to protect your family.
Thank you, Father, for believing in me.
Thank you for being you.
Father, I love you.*

You were with me in my darkest hour. You gave
me the power to make it through.
Dad, I love you.

March 8, 2018

Fear the Beast

Everything is fine. It is okay. Every time that is what he says.
There is a lesson to be learned, but you do not know what it is.
Do what you can so he does not get pissed.
He tells you not to lie, but it is your only way
out. You listen to him scream and shout.
That is better than the alternative. You do not forget or forgive.
There has got to be a better way to live.
You are playing ball, but he told you no. One
more roll and it gets out of control.

*Fear the beast. He is on the prowl. You shake
and shiver when you hear him howl.
Nowhere to run, it has begun. Nowhere to hide;
you are screaming for help inside.*

You think he is gone, but he is near. I tell you he can smell your fear.
You pray you make it through the night. Soon,
the beast will soothe his appetite.
The gig is up. You have been found. You
scream, but no one is around.
You pray for help. You pray to God. The
only answer you get is the rod.
One blow, two blows. You think how many more.
He smashes your head against the washing machine door.

*Fear the beast. He is on the prowl. You shake
and shiver when you hear him howl.
Nowhere to run, it has begun. Nowhere to hide;
you are screaming for help inside.*

You try to run, but don't get far. He drags you back by the hair.
Round two is about to begin.
It starts with a slap and ends with a kick.
The whole time you are thinking, *Someday, you fucking prick.*

The beast is full, and now he sleeps. He said
to be quiet and not to make a peep.
If he wakes, you know it too well; it is another trip back to hell.

July 24, 2017

Follow My Dreams

I am tired of being told what to do. I am
tired of being told where I can go.
I am tired of being a fool. I am tired of being told no.
I am tired of being told that I'm wrong
when I know that I am right.
I do not want to fight my whole life.
Oh god! There has to be a better way.
I am tired, and I can't take it anymore. No one
is looking escape through the door.

I want to escape. I got to break these chains.
I want to be free. Got to follow my dreams.
No more procrastination. I got to change my situation.
This time it is for me. It is time for me to be free.
It is time to follow my dreams.

Her name is Liberty. She is the prettiest lady that I have ever seen.
She gives me hope. She takes away my despair.
When I see her, it is like a breath of fresh air.
In my darkest times, she is a shining light.
She lets me know, with hard work, everything will be all right.

I want to escape. I got to break these chains.
I want to be free. Got to follow my dreams.
No more procrastination. I got to change my situation.
This time it is for me. It is time for me to be free.
It is time to follow my dreams.

She promises a brighter future, an escape from a struggling past.
It won't be easy, and it won't come fast.
I have to be patient. I have to bust my ass.
She makes me happy. She lets me be me. She
encourages me to be free and follow my dreams.

February 16, 2018

FOREVER YOUNG

People always say you are as young as you feel.
Lucky for me, my memories still seem real.
They say don't act like a child, be a man.
They can't feel the fire; they don't understand.
Their flame of youth has gone out.
The time has come; stand up and shout.
They tell me to act my age.
I tell them, "Break out of your cage."

Turn back the clock.
Life was a party that never stopped.
Hanging with my friends. Hoping the good times never end.
Eighteen and full of life. Laughing all day. Running wild in the night.
Forever young, we will always be. Reliving
the good times in my memory.

There, life is boring; it has no desire.
They need to break free and feel youth's fire.
As they grow old, their memories dwell in the shadow of
winter's cold. They need to feel the sun in their soul.
Put on your favorite record. Turn it up to ten.
Remember how it feels to be young again.
Too many people say I live in the past.
All I can say is kiss my ass.

Turn back the clock.
Life was a party that never stopped.
Hanging with my friends. Hoping the good times never end.
Eighteen and full of life. Laughing all day. Running wild in the night.
Forever young, we will always be. Reliving
the good times in my memory.

April 20, 1992

GREED

When is enough, enough? Never!
How long do I have to give? Forever!
I will be your friend until the end. How
much is in that bank account again?
Can you help me at the store? I need money
for gas; you need to give a little more.
Want to get a bite to eat? By the way, here is the receipt.
I just need one more than you; on second thought, make it two.

Money, money all I see. None for you, all for me.
Greed, greed everywhere. You have nothing, and I don't care.

I am going to fill my pockets with your last dime.
It won't take that much time.
I'm going to lie, cheat, and steal. Whatever it takes to seal the deal.

Money, money all I see. None for you, all for me.
Greed, greed everywhere. You have nothing, and I don't care.

When your account runs dry, that's when I say goodbye.
Do not worry, you will see me again.
Just one more time, my friend.
I will be there when you're dead, to steal the eyes out of your head.

Money, money all I see. None for you, all for me.
Greed, greed everywhere. You have nothing, and I don't care.

October 10, 2016

Highway of Life

As I travel down life's highway, I shed a tear and experience fears.
I am in search of a brighter day and a better
way with a spark of joy in my heart.
It brings memories to my mind of little boys chasing little girls.
Innocence is lost in the years. As I stop to rest, I see
friends growing older, and life getting colder.
As we grow wiser, life gets harder.
Life is a game of many riddles and few clues.
Do not try to figure it out, or you will lose.

*As life goes on, it gets much harder. Who has
the answers that I am looking for?
Give me the keys, and I will open the door.
With a strong heart and strong mind. The answers you will find.
It is all there; here is the key. Unlock your soul and let them be free.*

Life is full of problems, but no one has the answers.
We search for them, but it is all in vain. Life can be full of pain.
In life, we are born free. A slave only to time.
Time is our master. We play by its rules.
We live and die through time.

*As life goes on, it gets much harder. Who has
the answers that I am looking for?
Give me the keys, and I will open the door.
With a strong heart and strong mind. The answers you will find.
It is all there; here is the key. Unlock your soul and let them be free.*

As I continue my journey on the road of life, I see a vision of hope.
My family and friends are all there to greet me and spread cheer.
I see a light at the end of the tunnel. My
heart beats faster; it beats stronger.
The last mile is the longest. I now know the meaning of life.
Life is precious. Life is great. I am ready for
my maker. My soul he will take.

I know no wrong. I know no right. My
eyes have finally seen the light.
Going down life's highway.
A journey through time, through your mind.
Going down life's highway. Think of all the treasures you could find.

April 17, 1989

Hope for Help

At night, I close my eyes and slip into a lonely dream.
I find myself walking through the shadows
of my life. I want to scream.
Balancing what's wrong and right along the edge of a knife.
Careful not to fall. Why does it seem my
backs always up against the wall?
I cry out for help, but it's always far away, and I feel like a stranger
to myself. I feel the things I say and do aren't me but someone else.
I fall down on my knees and cry out for help.
Life is precious to us all. Like a newborn in
his growing years, I shed a tear.
As his life unfolds, his young hands turn to old.
If we could somehow turn back the hands on the clock,
Maybe my memories wouldn't be like waves crashing on the rocks.
Life is precious, but leaves too soon.
Somehow I missed that dance illuminated by the moon.
Now that it's the dying days, so many things
to say; let me count the ways.
All the mistakes I ever made.
I don't think the world would mind if I
turned back the hands of time.
To give me just one more chance and allow me to have that dance.
From a newborn to a man. You will crawl then stand.
Grab ahold of life and don't let go. Don't give up hope
or you will be left out in the cold. Lead a steady course.
Always search for the magic in the universe.
We are all on that merry-go-round. Reaching for the golden ring.
Don't let it pass you by. It's your choice. You're
more than a body with a voice. Shout it!
Help me find the land of hope!
Help me cruise in that boat!
Help me sail on the sea of life!
Help me! Don't get lost in the night.

Be strong, don't give up the good fight, and keep
on searching for the promised land. Hope, it seems
so very far. Never forget who you are.
Hope I see it in my sights.
Hope everything will be all right.
Hope it isn't far away.
Hope, listen to what I say.

1989

I Haven't Broken My Promise

Do you remember when we first met?
You were so eager, and I was playing hard to get.
Do you remember our first date?
We had a great time. I sent you flowers the next day.
I remember when you said I do. I also
remember my promise to you.

I promise to love you through the good times and bad.
Our love for each other is all we have.
I promise to keep you in my heart every day.
I promise my love for you will never stray.
I promise to hold you. I want to kiss your neck.
I haven't broken my promise yet.

Now we are older and a little grey.
I still love you every day.
Through all the years, through all the tears,
you are the light to calm my fears.

I promise to love you through the good times and bad.
Our love for each other is all we have.
I promise to keep you in my heart every day.
I promise my love for you will never stray.
I promise to hold you. I want to kiss your neck.
I haven't broken my promise yet.

Now you are gone. You never said goodbye.
I cannot count all the tears that fall from my eyes.
I miss you more in every way even though I talk to you every day.
I miss your laugh. I miss your touch. I miss your love, oh so much.

I promise to love you through the good times and bad.
Our love for each other is all we have.
I promise to keep you in my heart every day.

I promise my love for you will never stray.
I promise to hold you. I want to kiss your neck.
I haven't broken my promise yet.

January 19, 2018

King Greed

I have been around since the beginning of time.
I witnessed the birth of mankind.
I am everywhere, but you cannot see me. I whisper
in your ear. I know you can hear me.
I have taken from the strongest men. I have
disbanded the closest friends.
I have cut the bond of husband and wife. It was
like cutting soft butter with a hot knife.
I have conspired to take down empires. I know all
your desires. I am the spark for your fire.

I am your master. Worship me, come to me, and bend your knee.
I will promise you everything. It will cost you everything.
You know me; shout my name, for I am King Greed.

I have destroyed families, turned brother against brother.
Traded love of family, for the love of something other.
I will sneak into your mind and then your soul.
It will not be long until I have control.
A whisper here. A suggestion there. It will not
be long until my treasure is near.
You will lie for me and steal in my name.
I am the only winner in this game.
Now that I got all there was to get, I cast you aside with no regrets.
I took everything from you and left you alone. I
admire my trinkets while I sit on my throne.

I am your master. Worship me, come to me, and bend your knee.
I will promise you everything. It will cost you everything.
You know me; shout my name, for I am King Greed.

August 19, 2017

KRAMPUS

You waited all year for this night.
How can you be good when being bad feels so right?
You hung your stockings. You say your prayers.
You ask God for your soul he keeps.
You close your eyes and try to sleep.
What was that noise? Was it the wind? I don't know there it is again.
You hope it is Santa, bringing joy. You can't
wait to play with all your new toys.
You try to think of tomorrow's cheers. You try to erase all your fears.
There is that noise. Is it in your head? Maybe
you shoulda looked under the bed.

You waited all year for this night. Do you think
you will wake with the morning light?
Krampus is here. There is no coming back. He is
going to beat you and throw you in his sack.
Krampus is here. What can you do? The
nightmare is over, and so are you.
All the naughty boys and girls, he gathers them from around the world.
Now it is time for the feast. He will dine on your meat.
For he is Krampus the beast.

You thought no one seen you steal that candy. You
thought no one seen you push little Andy.
How can anybody know if you have been good or bad?
You laugh at all the fun you had.
Krampus knows. He has from the start.
He knows what evil lies in children's hearts.
So you better be good; there is no doubt.
That is the only way you can keep Krampus out.

You waited all year for this night. Do you think
you will wake with the morning light?

*Krampus is here. There is no coming back. He is
going to beat you and throw you in his sack.
Krampus is here. What can you do? The
nightmare is over, and so are you.
All the naughty boys and girls, he gathers them from around the world.
Now it is time for the feast. He will dine on your meat.
For he is Krampus the beast.*

January 20, 2018

LAND OF THE FREE?

Bodies fill the fields we plow. Blood will spill into the sea.
War is not a pretty thing. All it brings is misery.
Looking out for ourselves. Don't care about our fellow man.
Killing thousands to make a buck. I will never understand.
Killing for religion, that is so absurd. Tell me
when God said, "Kill thy fellow man?"
Politicians so corrupt, full of greed and lies. Bleeding
all the people until they hear them cry.
Look at all the preachers; see them on TV. Send your
money for God. I will make sure he gets it. Send it
straight to me. Our country is so great. Yes, it's true. But
can you tell me why are children have no food?

Land of the free. Home of the brave. Tell me, will we be saved?
Land of the free. Home of the brave. Tell me,
are we digging our own graves?

Polluting our air and sea does not make much sense to me.
Remember the tear in the Indian's eye? If
we don't stop, we will all truly die.
Telling people what to think and what to
say, that is not the American way.
It is our right to be free, and you will not take that away from me.

Land of the free. Home of the brave. Tell me, will we be saved?
Land of the free. Home of the brave. Tell me,
are we digging our own graves?

Our government is full of deceit and lies. Killing
democracy, can you hear its cries?
Land of the free and home of the brave.
The new American way. Do unto others before they do unto you.
Land of the free. Home of the brave. Who is free?

August 22, 1990

LEONARD

I am Leonard the Angry Dwarf. I will suck on your eyeballs.
I will eat your liver for the main course.
I am tiny, but make no mistake, I am pure evil.
I took a shit in your chocolate cake.
The kids say I am funny and want to play.
I will steal all your money and punch you in the face.
"Oh, Leonard, please show us a trick."
How about I pop your balloon with my prick.
I'm so tired of this yellow brick road. I'll wait for
you to pass, then I will slit your throat.
I am not looking for a pot of gold.
Someone, get me a ladder. I'm going to fuck your bunghole.
You might think this is silly or even a joke.
But I'm about to free Willy, and you're about to choke.
I will walk up to you and let you know.
There is a new king in town. Get off my throne.
You can polish my knob, then you can polish my crown.
Ha! Ha! Ha! You think I'm a clown.
I'll bite your ankles. I will bring you down.
You're a big guy, calling me a small fry.
But I like eating pie. That is why I am between your girl's thighs.
Leonard. Oh, Leonard. You can hear her scream.
You are the dwarf of my dreams.

April 27, 1999

Living Again

What happened to the plans we made?
They say, in time, the pain fades.
Can you tell me how?
How to replace this empty space.
When everywhere I see your face, it is an image that I can't erase.

I saw your face again. I heard your voice in the wind.
This isn't how I wanted our story to end.
Hit rewind, and it's back to the beginning.
I see your face again. I hear your voice in the wind.
I stop for a moment and grin.
Then it's back to the living again.

From the start, we had big dreams.
That was a lifetime ago, or so it seems.
I fell on my knees and begged for healing, but
now I'm left with empty feelings.
I can't find the answers to my questions.
It seems like everyone has a suggestion.
No matter how hard I try.
I just can't find a reason why.
What do I do? Where do I go from here?
In this empty bed, I drown in my tears.

I saw your face again. I heard your voice in the wind.
This isn't how I wanted our story to end.
Hit rewind, and it's back to the beginning.
I see your face again. I hear your voice in the wind.
I stop for a moment and grin.
Then it's back to the living again.

The pain doesn't fade.
I still talk to you every day.
I know you're gone, but I remember you when I hear that song.

You still come up in conversations and probably
will until I reach my destination.
Ever since we have been apart,
I have been slowly dying of a broken heart.
It makes me sad, feeling all alone, but I know
I'll see you when I come home.

April 22, 2021

Long Way Home

Ripped away from your family.
Sent away and viewed as the enemy.
All you want to do is help.
How did you end up in this hell?
It is not your fight, but you do what you are told.
You do what is right.
Try to stay low and out of sights.
Bullets flying by your head.
Oh my god, Tommy is dead!
Running and hiding. They just hit Craig.
There's an explosion. Timmy can't feel his legs.

It's a long way home tonight. You pray for the angel's guiding light.
The wounds of war run so deep. These scars you will always keep.
The screams will not let you sleep.
It's a long way home tonight.
You just want to see your family one last time.
You pray to God that you don't die.

You radio for help. They say they are coming.
Ammo is low, next to nothing.
You are surrounded, nowhere to go.
Your throat is so dry you want to choke.
You got to think fast. You need a plan.
You are responsible for the safety of every man.
You can't move snipers all around.
How are you going to get out of this fucking town?

It's a long way home tonight. You pray for the angel's guiding light.
The wounds of war run so deep. These scars you will always keep.
The screams will not let you sleep.
It's a long way home tonight.
You just want to see your family one last time.
You pray to God that you don't die.

Stuck on a roof on Black Sunday. Praying
someone comes to your aide.
Soon morning turns to night. They could
not see our light in the night.
You burn the shirts off your backs.
Hoping the Bradlys and Charlie join the attack.
Dodging bullets. Running through your fear.
Yelling and praying that someone will hear.
You catch the attention of a tank. You fall
on your knees and give thanks.
Now you are safe, and so are your men.
You get to see your family again.

It's a long way home tonight. You pray for the angel's guiding light.
The wounds of war run so deep. These scars you will always keep.
The screams will not let you sleep.
It's a long way home tonight.
You just want to see your family one last time.
You pray to God that you don't die.

July 4, 2019

LOST

I woke up this morning and something was wrong.
I searched everywhere, but it was gone.
I looked in the closet and under the bed.
Was there something I could have done to stop it?
Now I am full of dread.
Did I have it in the car?
I hope it is not very far.

It's lost. It's lost.
I want it back, and I will pay any cost.
People tell me to calm down. It's okay.
I don't care what they say.
It's lost. It's lost.
Where can it be?
Do you understand what it is doing to me?

Have you seen it? Did you take it?
Are you amused? I got to get it back before it is abused.

It's lost. It's lost.
I want it back, and I will pay any cost.
People tell me to calm down. It's okay.
I don't care what they say.
It's lost. It's lost.
Where can it be?
Do you understand what it is doing to me?

I don't understand it. I am not blind, but I can't find it.
This feeling is so unkind. Can someone
please help me locate my mind?

It's lost. It's lost.
I want it back, and I will pay any cost.
People tell me to calm down. It's okay.
I don't care what they say.

It's lost. It's lost.
Where can it be?
Do you understand what it is doing to me?

May 2, 2018

MEANT TO BE

Nothing special when we met. I guess the
magic had not happened yet.
But as time went by, you caught my eye.
I was drunk, and you were shy.
When we went out with our friends, who
knew how the night would end.
You lost your keys. A damsel in distress.
So I did what I do best, and as they say, history knows the rest.

We were meant to be together.
We promised our love forever. We sealed it with a kiss.
Still remember those soft lips.
That is when two became one, and soon three became one.
We were meant to be together, and we will forever.

All day long, I sit and wait. I am picturing the perfect date.
What can I do? I need to be with you.
What will I wear? What will I say? Will I take your breath away?
Now I can't stop thinking of you.
You are on my mind.
There, you are looking so fine.
Oh, how I hunger for your touch.
Hunger. Anticipation of your kiss.
The separation is just too much.
It is your love that I miss.
One day, I will take that flight, and we will reunite.

We were meant to be together.
We promised our love forever. We sealed it with a kiss.
Still remember those soft lips.
That is when two became one, and soon three became one.
We were meant to be together, and we will forever.

June 1, 2018

Mother, Sweet Mother

Dedicated to Florence Patistea

You gave me life, and I can never pay you back for that.
You taught me to speak, and all I can say
is I love you unconditionally.
You tied my shoes, and whenever you need
me, I will come running back for you.
You held my hand. You helped me to stand. You
helped me to walk. You taught me to talk.

Mother, sweet Mother, I want you to know.
You are with me everywhere that I go.
Mother, sweet Mother, you are more than a friend.
Saying I love you is where I will begin.
Mother, sweet Mother, my love for you will never end.

When I woke at night, you were my shining light.
You dried my tears. You chased away all my fears.
You locked the boogeyman up real tight
and made sure that I was all right.

Mother, sweet Mother, I want you to know.
You are with me everywhere that I go.
Mother, sweet Mother, you are more than a friend.
Saying I love you is where I will begin.
Mother, sweet Mother, my love for you will never end.

You taught me to say thank you and please.
You wiped the blood from my knees.
You were the tissue when I sneezed.
You made me the best me that I could be.

Mother, sweet Mother, I want you to know.
You are with me everywhere that I go.

Mother, sweet Mother, you are more than a friend.
Saying I love you is where I will begin.
Mother, sweet Mother, my love for you will never end.

July 24, 2017

When I Am Gone

I just want to be happy. Living in society.
Living the way my momma taught me.
She said, "Boy, listen up before my time is up.
Have a couple of kids. Find a good woman to be your wife.
That is the recipe for a perfect life."
We never saw that truck coming. All we heard was the crash.
Smelled the screeching tires and felt the broken glass.
When I awoke, I choked on the smoke.
There were three white sheets lying in the road.
No one's going to miss me when I'm gone.
Momma, your recipe was wrong. Now, at the
end, the bottle is my only friend.
It has been three weeks since the wreck.
They found me with the rope around my neck.
Suzy was a bright girl. She was the star in her family's world.
She was a good kid. Not many friends.
She was so excited when Billy gave her that bracelet
for her wrist. Then he sealed it with a kiss.
He invited her to a party. It soon got out of hand.
Billy took her innocence and became a man.
They put it on the internet. They said it was a joke.
That was the day her heart broke.
It felt like a kick in the gut. Every time they called her slut.
They said they meant no harm. When they found her
with a needle in her arm and a note that read:
"No one's going to miss me when I'm gone.
I tried to live life right, but I am tired of losing this fight.
No one's going to miss me when I'm gone."

November 17, 2017

No Tears for Me

You hear it all the time. If only I had seen the signs.
I tried to show you, but you were blind.
You said that we would talk at another time.
Is it pride, or is it shame?
I need your help because I'm losing this game.
Don't have the answers, can't find a clue.
I'm so confused. I'm so sorry. I didn't mean to bother you.
I'm surrounded by darkness. There is no light.
It's the last round, and I'm too tired to fight.

There is no hope at the end of my rope.
Bullet, blade, or pills?
My fire is dying, and I got the chills.
Standing on the ledge. Waiting for a call.
Begging for a reason not to jump because one more step, and I'll fall.
No tears for me. Is it fear that is stopping me, or
are my demons not through with me?
No tears for me. Don't you cry. Given another
chance, would you find the time?
No tears for me. I'm finally free; with open arms, they welcome me.

I don't know where he came from.
I just needed a friend, and he was there right to the end.
Full of anxiety. Full of depression.
He didn't judge. He just listened to my confessions.
Whispering in my ear, "Listen to me. I'll take away all of your fears."
I reached out to you all.
I got back, not even one call.
So sorry to bother you. I don't know what else to do.
Still waiting for a call, my back is against the wall.

There is no hope at the end of my rope.
Bullet, blade, or pills?
My fire is dying, and I got the chills.

Standing on the ledge. Waiting for a call.
Begging for a reason not to jump because one more step, and I'll fall.
No tears for me. Is it fear that is stopping me, or
are my demons not through with me?
No tears for me. Don't you cry. Given another
chance, would you find the time?
No tears for me. I'm finally free; with open arms, they welcome me.

He no longer whispers. Now he yells.
He tells me that he can save me from this hell.
I can't take the pounding in my head.
I'm so tired, and he offers me his bed.
I'm so lonely. So depressed. I can no longer
hold back the walls of stress.
I'm so tired. Just need to rest.
Should I take his advice? Maybe he knows best.

There is no hope at the end of my rope.
Bullet, blade, or pills?
My fire is dying, and I got the chills.
Standing on the ledge. Waiting for a call.
Begging for a reason not to jump because one more step, and I'll fall.
No tears for me. Is it fear that is stopping me, or
are my demons not through with me?
No tears for me. Don't you cry. Given another
chance, would you find the time?
No tears for me. You better not cry. With my last breath, I say goodbye.

February 25, 2021

ON THE CORNER

When I saw you on the corner, I knew it had to be.
So I walked up to you, and you told me, "Baby, you and me for a fee.
Baby, you and me, but this ride is not free."

When you pass me by, I struggle to say hi.
Your beauty blinds my eyes.
In your high heels and your short skirt, you look fine.
I love to look at your warm soft hair. Your perfume fills the air.

When I saw you on the corner, I knew it had to be.
So I walked up to you, and you told me, "Baby, you and me for a fee.
Baby, you and me, but this ride is not free."

You seemed so innocent and so nice. I was
guilty. I had lust in my eyes.
You're all I want. You're all I need.
Will you be mine? Baby, I will for a dime.
You look so sweet. A treat I would like to eat.
I don't want to be like Rocky, beating the meat.

When I saw you on the corner, I knew it had to be.
So I walked up to you, and you told me, "Baby you and me for a fee.
Baby, you and me, but this ride is not free."

I found love. Now I got to find a glove.
Now it is hard and time for you to part.
I am ready to start, but I am done.
I got no money and no fun.

When I saw you on the corner, I knew it had to be.
So I walked up to you, and you told me, "Baby, you and me for a fee.
Baby, you and me, but this ride is not free."

June 18, 1988

OPPOSITES

You like to plan.
I like to wing it.
You want to rap, and I want to sing it.
You like to walk.
I want to run.
Have some faith and jump with me.
Spread your arms and feel what it is like to be free.
We can fly like Icarus before he gets too close to the sun.
Now our hearts beat as one.

Do you remember watching that movie?
You grabbed my hand when you got scared.
But I remember you holding me tightly. Chasing away my fears.
Do you remember getting lost and making out in the van?
You asked me if we could make it, and I told you we can.
They say opposites attract, and now I know that it is a fact.
We go together like foot and glove.
But it is easy when you are in love.

I want to stay.
You want to go.
I move fast, and you go slow.
I want to eat in.
You want to eat out.
Compromise is what it is all about.
I wake early.
You sleep late.
Together forever is our fate.

Do you remember watching that movie?
You grabbed my hand when you got scared.
But I remember you holding me tightly. Chasing away my fears.
Do you remember getting lost and making out in the van?
You asked me if we could make it, and I told you we can.

They say opposites attract, and now I know that it is a fact.
We go together like foot and glove.
But it is easy when you are in love.

July 4, 2019

PLAINS OF WAR

At first, there were tribes; do you know what I mean?
Comanche and Cherokee. The Cheyenne. The Sioux.
The white man came and told them they had to move.
The land was theirs by birthright, but we came ready to fight.
We told them that we came in peace, but
they saw through our deceit.
General Custer and the seventh advanced on
Chief Black Kettle and the Washita.
The plan was to send them all to heaven.
The old and the young, we hear your pleas. We ignore your cries.
We leave them all dead, covered in flies.

*Lightning has struck on the Great Plains, and as you
can see, the night begins to bleed in the rain.
We are on the plains of war. It was started with false words.
Can you feel the pains of war? We fight until there is no more.*

We sent our best soldiers to fight their
strongest and bravest warriors.
They had knives. We had swords.
We tried to trick them with empty words.
They had arrows. We had guns. The Battle
of Little Big Horn has begun.

*Lightning has struck on the Great Plains, and as you
can see, the night begins to bleed in the rain.
We are on the plains of war. It was started with false words.
Can you feel the pains of war? We fight until there is no more.*

When we sent General Custer and the seventh to fight the red
man, we did not know that it would be his last stand. We thought
that General Custer had won, but reinforcements were near.
The battle was done. They attacked from the rear.
They fought strong. They were brave. There was too
many Indians, and no soldiers were saved.

The battle was a classic. All the soldiers came back in caskets.

*Lightning has struck on the Great Plains, and as you
can see, the night begins to bleed in the rain.
We are on the plains of war. It was started with false words.
Can you feel the pains of war? We fight until there is no more.*

All the white men knew they were disgraced. The
Indians did not give up. The rage was too great.
The reinforcements finally arrived. We found out
General Custer and his men did not survive.
They killed the warriors. They raped their wives. The Indians
had crimson in our eyes. The Indians left none alive.

*Lightning has struck on the Great Plains, and as you
can see, the night begins to bleed in the rain.
We are on the plains of war. It was started with false words.
Can you feel the pains of war? We fight until there is no more.*

May 10, 1988

Public Enemy No. 1

Wake up, it is not time for dreaming. You better start screaming.
Who turned out the lights? I cannot believe
what happened last night.
There I was, out on the streets, hungry for fresh meat.
Anticipating your every move, while you
were getting into the groove.
You looked hot out on the dance floor, shaking what you got.
You thought you were smart. You thought you were
cool, turning the guys into drooling little fools.
You came up to me and asked me my name. You
thought you were a master of this game.
Baby, now you met your match. How could
you know that I would be your last?
You looked good, so you took a chance.
You asked me to buy you a drink and a dance.
You use your looks for your gain. Another
man's heart you filled with pain.
Now you are mine. You are in my control.
It is my will, not your own.
I will take you down so fast; baby, tonight, you breathe your last.
Do not try to run or escape. You know it is just too late.
My eyes are filled with hate. It is time for you to meet your fate.
As my hands closed tight around your throat,
do not try to fight. There is no way out.
A victim, you have become of public enemy number 1.
You tried to hide. You tried to run.

I am a master of this game, and it has begun.
You let out a scream. Are we having fun?
You are the victim of public enemy number 1.

You left the husband and kids home tonight.
You told them you love them and not to
wait because you had to work late.

You fixed your hair. Your dress is tight. You got
your high heels on, looking for Mr. Right.
Here I am, sitting at the bar. You ask me to buy you a drink
as you pull up a seat. I just want to be alone. I do not want to
hear you speak, but you tell me it is time for another drink.
You say this is your favorite song. You pick up
your dress and show me your thong.
Soon, you will be leaving with Mr. Wrong. A
kiss on the neck. A caress of the skin.
Now it is time for my work to begin.
A whisper in your ear. Down your cheek, runs a single tear.
A slice of my knife. You do not realize I just took your life.
The game is over. I have won. You are another
victim of public enemy number 1.
You tried to hide. You tried to run.

I am a master of this game, and it has begun.
You let out a scream. Are we having fun?
You are the victim of public enemy number 1.

August 27, 2017

PUERTO RICO

Brandin, Josh, and Mike packed a bag and jumped on a flight.
We were going on vacation, and Puerto Rico was the destination.
Gracias to my boy Josh for showing us around his home soil.

Reyes del dia. Happy hour and having fun.
Reyes del dia. We were baking in the sun.
Reyes del dia. We were drinking Gasolina.
Having fun in Puerto Rico, there is no better feeling.

Going to Abuela's for some food.
Drinking Medalla to get us in the mood.
Going to Church for our first feast
Riding jet skis in the sea.
Watching the beautiful *chicas* on the street.

Reyes del dia. Happy hour and having fun.
Reyes del dia. We were baking in the sun.
Reyes del dia. We were drinking Gasolina.
Having fun in Puerto Rico, there is no better feeling.

Eating *quenepas* and cruising all day.
Chilling at night. Enjoying life and feeling all right.
Celebrating the fort with thirteen miles.
Breaking the rules and laughing until we were crying.
We see *muchas chicas herosas.*
Give a wink and crack a smile.
Puerto Rico, all we can say is, "*Gracias, adios, mucho amore.*"

August 6, 2016

Rock and Roll

I got the music flowing through my soul. You
know it has got to be rock and roll.
I turn the volume all the way up to ten. You
know our music has got no end.
We listen to the songs again and again.
Driving in the car or walking the dog.
Our music makes us happy. How could it be wrong?
Riding a horse or chasing a goose. It doesn't matter what you do.
It just matters what you are listening to.
So just put on that rock and roll. It will go right to your soul.
Your hands and feet start to tap.
Soon, you forget all your life's crap.
The lyrics come to your mind, and the tune is not so hard to find.
So work, rest, or play. You know what I say.
Rock and roll is good for your mind and good for the soul.
Don't try to fight it; just let it take control.
You tell me that I am wasting my time and
that our music ought to be a crime.
But just like the colonies, a long time ago, fighting
for their independence as we all know.
We will fight for our rock and roll.
Because we love it when it touches our soul.
We love it when it takes control because
it is that crazy rock and roll.

May 5, 1988

Secret Man

People walk down the street. Fearing all the people they may meet.
All the crime in our town, bringing everybody down.
Cops are stuck; the law is screwed. Mr. Mayor, what are we to do?
Look in the sky. What do you see? He is coming closer to me.
It is a secret man. It's a secret man.
Secret Man, who are you? Secret Man, who are you?
Since he came, crime is down. People no longer frown.
All the kids look up to him. Someday, they will be like him.
A Secret Man.
Then one day, he went away. Crime was getting worse day by day.
Kids were afraid to play in the street.
People afraid of people they meet.
Cops are stuck. The law is screwed. Mr. Mayor, what are we to do?
Secret Man, where are you? Secret Man, we need you.
Secret Man, our savior. Secret Man, our hero.
Secret Man, where are you? Secret Man, we need you.

April 27, 1988

SWEET INNOCENCE

There goes the man that stole you from me.
I'm not blind, but I didn't see.
He came like a thief in the night. He offered
friendship and said it is all right.
How could he destroy something so innocent and sweet?
There goes the motherfucker laughing at me.
He bought you trinkets. He bought you food.
He said, "It is our little secret. Everything is cool."
He followed you from the park. It was just about getting dark.
He said you are a special girl. He is going
to take you around the world.
He is going to take you to places you've never
been. He said you are his special friend.
You were my baby. I should have been there. Do
you know how it is to face your worst fears?
You were just twelve years old. Funny Uncle
Harold is what he was called.
He got you in his van. Now it is time for his evil plan.
He gave you a drink to get you lose. Then
he pulled down your underoos.
He said, "Relax, this won't hurt." Then he
tied your hands with his shirt.
Snap, crackle, pop as you scream for him to stop.
There is no hero with a cape. You try to
break free, but there is no escape.
Now the monster is done. He says, "Now wasn't
that fun? Go home, child. Run!"
You tell no one. Try to hide the shame.
Try to delete it from your brain.
Then one day, your secret comes out.
He gets arrested. There is a trial. He sits
there the whole time with a smile.
They let him go on a technicality. He is
back on the streets, roaming free.

There goes the motherfucker that stole you from me.
I pull out my gun. He says, "No! Please. I am sorry."
I tell him, "This will be fun, not to worry."
I tell him. "You should not have stolen her from me.
You stole her innocence. She was so sweet."
He says, "You can have her. She meant nothing to me."
There was a flash. There was a bang. Now I laugh as you bleed.

December 4, 2017

THE BEAST

What have you done to deserve this fate?
Better run before it's too late.
Adrenaline pumping through his veins, making him go insane.
Fed by anger, driven by hate.
Here comes the anger; there's no escape.

The beast feeds well tonight.
Devouring everything in sight.
It will hunt until it finds its prey—it grows larger every day.
It feels no mercy, guilt, or shame.
You cannot simply wish it away.

He told you to stop, but you wouldn't listen.
Releasing the beast has become his mission.
The transformation has begun.
There is no turning back; you better run.
There is no bargaining with this beast.
You've done your crime; now he is unleashed.
The chase is on you; better run for your life.
The first strike comes and it's like getting slashed with a knife.
It doesn't matter if you beg him to stop; on the second strike,
you hear a pop. You can't run, so you start to crawl.
He picks you up and slams you into the wall.
You try to catch your breath while you cry.
Your heart is racing, and your throat is dry.
You think it is over, but it just began.
You try to get away when he says, "Let's have some fun."

The beast feeds well tonight.
Devouring everything in sight.
It will hunt until it finds its prey; it grows larger every day.
It feels no mercy, guilt, or shame.
You cannot simply wish it away.

Another hit, another slap. A pull of the hair and all that crap.
You pray to God to help you now.
You wish you were someone else—somewhere, somehow.
Then you see it in his eyes. The beast is full. The anger dies.

The beast feeds well tonight.
Devouring everything in sight.
It will hunt until it finds its prey—it grows larger every day.
It feels no mercy, guilt, or shame.
You cannot simply wish it away.

Your body lies in the night, broken and bleeding from the fight.
The beast escapes with the light.
He's not gone, just asleep. Be careful not to make a peep.
If he wakes, you are doomed. A shell of
a man creeps into your room.
Caresses your hand and whispers to you,
"Why did you make me do it? I love you."

The beast feeds well tonight.
Devouring everything in sight.
It will hunt until it finds its prey—it grows larger every day.
It feels no mercy, guilt, or shame.
You cannot simply wish it away.

2008

THE BOYS

It has been so long since we have been apart.
I don't know why you tried to break my heart.
I am so tired of being alone. I am so tired of staying at home.
I pick up the phone, and I take a chance.
It is time to get back into the dance.
I am calling my boys to see what is up.
We are not coming home until the sun comes up.

We are going to make some noise and have some fun.
I am going out with the boys. We are going to raise some hell.
The night is young.
We are going to fly. Find a pretty girl that will help me touch the sky.

Brunette, blonde, and redhead—watching
them dance is quite pleasing.
We have another drink while they keep teasing.
Talking and laughing. Having fun. The
hunt for Mrs. Right has begun.
There she is. This is no joke. I tell the boys and go for broke.

I am going out with the boys. We are going to raise some hell.
We are going to make some noise and have some fun.
The night is young.
We are going to fly. Find a pretty girl that will help me touch the sky.

Now it is time to play the game. I go over and ask her name.
We laugh and flirt. She looks good in her skirt.
Eyes on the prize. She gives me a rise.
We both are feeling good. If I ask, I wonder if she would.
If everything goes all right, she will be
coming home with me tonight.
What a night. I will never forget it. I hope
I don't do anything to regret it.

August 21, 1988

The Edge of Reality

Alone in my world, nothing seems to bother me.
If you only knew the feelings that I feel.
Alone in my world, I feel so safe. All the visions in
my mind are all the horrors you will find.
When you sleep and dream and are awakened by the
screams, is it real or fantasy? Who is lost? Who is saved?
I envision a lonely grave. Will you fall on your knees and pray?
Who is to say? What is wrong or right? Will we ever find the light?

On the edge of reality, is it real or fantasy?
On the edge of reality, who is lost? Who is saved?
Each day that goes by is another loss.
Each day that goes by, we pay the ultimate cost.

In my mind, I am king. I sit on a lonely throne. Why
are you destroying me? You will never take my crown.
Only the strong prevail; all the others fail.
In my kingdom, I am strong; on the edge
of reality is where I belong.

On the edge of reality, is it real or fantasy?
On the edge of reality, who is lost? Who is saved?
Each day that goes by is another loss.
Each day that goes by, we pay the ultimate cost.

If you're lost, don't be afraid; take my hand; I will show you the way.
But if you pose a threat to me, you truly will taste defeat.
You won't see me coming. You won't hear a sound.
You won't feel it until it's too late. I'll crush you in the ground.
That is why I wear the crown.
You might think I'm crazy; that's all right by me.
That's why I live on the edge of reality.

*On the edge of reality, that's where you'll be.
On the edge of reality, it has no boundaries.
On the edge of reality, it's all in the mind.
On the edge of reality, think of all the horrors you will find.
On the edge of reality, I am your king.
On the edge of reality, you are mine.
On the edge of reality, you will never leave.
On the edge of reality, you will die.*

1989

FORGOTTEN ONE

The call for war is loud and strong.
Our young boys go proud; nothing seems wrong.
Soon this boy will be a man. On the battlefield, he will stand.
Fights with love and honor for his homeland.
Blood will shed and not just his own.
Don't want to fight anymore; just want to go home.
Cries in the night for fear of his life.
Can you hear the screams in the night?
No time for fear; the enemy is near.
What can you do? What can you say? Only got a second to pray.
He sees his buddy blown away.
War has no allies. Nothing left to say.

Can you hear him cry in the night for fear of his life?
Hear the explosions blinded by the light.
No time to fear; the enemy is near.
The forgotten one.

War is done, and who has won? The old soldier stares at the sun.
He came back, but everything is not all right. He
still hears the bombs and screams in the night.
Society cast him aside; now he is forced into the shadows and hides.
Got no money because he can't get a job.
There, he was a hero. Here, they call him a slob.

Can you hear him cry in the night for fear of his life?
Hear the explosions blinded by the light.
No time to fear; the enemy is near.
The forgotten one.

The scars of war run so deep. He is there while you sleep.
The flashbacks are really strong.
Society still sees nothing wrong.
Society has cast him out; is this what this world is all about?

Remembering all the bloody scenes. This
goes on while he tries to sleep.
He is still fighting an enemy. Losing the battle for his sanity.

Can you hear him cry in the night for fear of his life?
Hear the explosions blinded by the light.
No time to fear; the enemy is near.
The forgotten one.

He gave his life for us all. He saw his comrades fall.
Over there, he was great. Back here, nothing but hate.
Every day he loses the fight. Can't take it anymore. Takes his life.
He is the forgotten one.

1990

THE GREAT PLAINS

The white man came for our land, and from the
shake of the hand, we offered them peace.
They just gave us deceit. They push us
west and tell us it is for the best.
We thought it's fair to share the land, but they
wanted more and more gold to pan.
They raped our women, slaughtered our
child, and they call us wild?
Tensions build. Pain in the heart. We are finally ready for our attack.
Lakota, Cheyenne, and Sioux—what were they supposed to do?
They had guns and swords forged from
steel. We had arrows and spears.
No longer would we kneel.

*War has come to the great plains. The fight rages on and on.
We fight for our way of life. How can we be
wrong? The fight goes on and on.*

We retreat to the Black Hills. When they
come, we will be ready to kill.
They sent General Custer and the seventh. They
tried to retreat, but we wouldn't let them.
Crazy horse and sitting bull, their anger and rage was full.
Never was their wisdom dull.
They made a plan to take back their land.
Some people said the Battle of Little Big Horn was a classic.
General Custer and 268 of his men went home in caskets.

*War has come to the great plains. The fight rages on and on.
We fight for our way of life. How can we be
wrong? The fight goes on and on.*

The victor we will never be. The scars of war run too deep.

April 17, 1989

THE LONELY TRAIN

I am so lonely every night, and something is
missing; it just does not seem right.
The rain is falling. I can hear you calling.
It will not be long, just one more song.
I am missing you every night. I want to hold
you in my arms and squeeze you tight.

I am on that lonely train home tonight. I know
you are going to make everything all right.
I am on that lonely train home tonight. I can
see your face in the neon lights.
It is such a long way home tonight. I count the miles until I am there.
You will kiss away all my tears.

Another night, another place. A thousand
smiles, but I only see your face.
I miss your smile. You drive me wild.
Searching for a way home, I guess I have to settle for the phone.
Another delay means a longer stay.
Searching for a reason to smile, it's like
searching for a lost little child.
I want your love, and I want it now. I wish I could
always be with you, but I do not know how.
Please do not shed a tear because I am almost there.
I cannot wait to get back to you because I know you care.

I am on that lonely train home tonight. I know
you are going to make everything all right.
I am on that lonely train home tonight. I can
see your face in the neon lights.
It is such a long way home tonight. I count the miles until I am there.
You will kiss away all my tears.

Ladylove guides my thoughts. I should be with you, but I am not.
Everything will be all right because I will be kissing you tonight.

August 6, 2012

The Man with No Eyes

There is a story that I must tell
As I lay in my dark and lonely cell.
I judge not you, but myself, as I live inside my hell.
I can't hide from the thoughts in my mind as I wait here to die.
Fifteen years ago, I killed a family. I sat and watched them die.
They thought that they were perfect, but they were living a lie.
People want to know why?
You don't even know them, so why do you cry?
Society labels me insane and sentences me to death.
But only I can feel my pain with each passing breath.
My soul is black. You can't see. I don't want anyone next to me.
Tell me, can you hear the screams?

You think you have taken everything from me.
You left me shackled on my knees.
To break my spirit, you take my eyes.
I still see the pictures in my mind.
I see the blood. I hear the screaming.
You say this is a nightmare, but I am not sleeping.

In life, we are created equal. No one better. No one worse.
Even when we are lying in that hearse.
Wake up! This is not a dream. I know you
would like to see me on my knees.
You want me begging for my life.
Who gave you the right to decide whether I live or whether I die?
Your life is one big hypocritical lie.

You think you have taken everything from me.
You left me shackled on my knees.
To break my spirit, you take my eyes.
I still see the pictures in my mind.
I see the blood. I hear the screaming.
You say this is a nightmare, but I am not sleeping.

I am the man with no eyes. I see everything as it be.
I see clearer than you ever will.
You judge me, but you can't wait for me to be killed.
You say your heart is heavy. Well, my mind is at ease.
Go now. Let me have some peace.
The final hour has come. Now I know my life is done.
I am the man with no eyes. I sit and listen as the world goes by.
Oh, I am not insane. Can you not hear the cries?

January 27, 1989

THE PROFITS OF WAR

Here they stand, face-to-face.
Are they trying to destroy the whole human race?
Fighting for honor, money, and land.
They were strong. They took their stand.
Drafting the boys and taking their toys.
Giving them guns and making them kill for someone else's funds.
Promises are made, but not one is kept.
We tell them that it is for the good of the empire.
Never shoot until you hear fire.
The war has started. Hate rages on.
The soldiers, they fight for all that is wrong.
The war is long. It last for years.
Many have fallen. Many shed tears.
The war is over. The politician's pockets have grown.
The soldier's honor and bravery has shown.
They come back for their reward.
For this is what we have heard.
Now the truth will finally come out.
That they have fought for another's greed.
It was such an evil deed.
The politician's words were full of deceit.
Oh, what an unholy feat.
Now it replays in their mind while they sleep.
He stands there with a smile and promises help.
He says you all served him well.
He knows you will never escape this hell.

May 4, 1989

THE RINGING IN MY HEAD

Constantly, all day long, not sure what exactly went wrong.
In the mirror, when I stare, it leaves me cold and shaking with fear.
There it stands; is it a man? I don't like what I see.
This ugliness staring back at me.
So annoying. So abusive. It makes me sick. So repulsive.

And I can't stop this ringing in my head. In my head. In my head.
This ringing in my head.
"Someone has got to pay." That is what it said.
Blood on the walls. Blood on the floor.
My work is done, and the ringing is no more.

There he is, dark as night. Assuring me everything is all right.
There he is. With his evil grin. Full of glee. Full of sin.
Whispering to me, "This has got to end."
Helping my anger grow, here comes the fear and the cold.

And I can't stop this ringing in my head. In my head. In my head.
This ringing in my head.
"Someone has got to pay." That is what it said.
Blood on the walls. Blood on the floor.
My work is done, and the ringing is no more.

I feel so strange. I am full of rage. I want
to break out of this fucking cage.
The transformation has taken place. You can
run, but you will not win this race.

And I can't stop this ringing in my head. In my head. In my head.
This ringing in my head.
"Someone has got to pay." That is what it said.
Blood on the walls. Blood on the floor.
My work is done, and the ringing is no more.

October 26, 1992

THE SWORD

Years went by. Our land had no king.
The bells of peace would no longer ring.
Anarchy and chaos, there was no law.
The people were in disarray.
What did we do that was so wrong?
The acts of war raged throughout the land.
Our darkest hour is now at hand.
But hidden away, through the town and in the woods,
There was a mighty noble sword. In a stone, it stood.
Waiting to be drawn from the stone
So a king can sit on the throne.
Year after year, mighty warriors try.
They all ended up sitting around to cry.
The priests cry out in prayer,
With hopes that their god will hear.
They beg their god to send them someone who would
know how to take the sword out of the stone
And take his rightful place on the throne.
It does not matter how strong. It does not matter how smart.
All that matters is if you are pure of heart.
Then one day, there was a boy.
He pulled the sword. How quickly spread the word.
The people knew joy.
The bells of peace again would ring.
The people, the land, once again had a king.

May 15, 1988

TIRED EYES

As I lay me down to sleep, I pray my soul God will keep.
I looked through my old tired eyes, and I wonder why.
Why is the world not clean?
What happened to society?
Why are people so mean?
What happened to our field of dreams?
I remember a time when people would care. Life seemed so fair.
But now all that has changed and no one gives a damn anymore.
What the hell should I care for?
You hear it all the time.
The world is going way too fast. How can you have peace of mind?
What happened to society? Where is the field of dreams?
Someday, I know we will find it. But right now,
it seems like people really don't give a shit.
How come good friends don't stay? Please, listen to what I say.
Do not go through life without a friend. You should
have one before the world comes to an end.
You live in love. If you are not married, people say it is a sin.
Why do so many lose yet so few win?
People on the street selling crack. They
don't really know where it is at.
Anything to make a buck. They don't care who
they hurt because they don't give a fuck.
People can change. Yes, it is true.
Make it a better world for you.
It is too late for me. Can't you see?
As I sit in the great palace in the sky, I looked
down with my tired old eyes.
I wonder what will happen to society.
Will you ever reach the field of dreams?
It seems so close, yet it is so far away.
Your grasp slips more and more every day. If people
don't change now, it will truly slip away.

April 21, 1988

Under the Blade

Welcome to my office.
Don't you think it is nice?
Why don't you take a number? You are the next sacrifice.
I am the doctor. I have the cure. Once you
step in, I will lock the door.
Nothing to fill out. Nothing to sign. You
will never get out. You are mine.

Under my blade, that is where I want you.
Under the blade, I will cut and slice you.
Under my blade, you are mine to control.
Under the blade, there is nowhere you can go.

No anesthesia. You will feel the pain when
I do a lobotomy on your brain.
I cut you once. I cut you twice. I cut you
again because it makes me feel nice.
Inflicting pain is my drug. I am addicted. I can't get enough.

Under my blade, that is where I want you.
Under the blade, I will cut and slice you.
Under my blade, you are mine to control.
Under the blade, there is nowhere you can go.

Now that I got you on my table.
You want to scream, but you are unable.
I tie you down with my restraints. Tell me, does
the sight of blood make you faint?
It is almost over. The pain you will feel. This is not a nightmare.
This is real. No need for stitches or a pill.
I will take your life to pay the bill.

Under my blade, that is where I want you.
Under the blade, I will cut and slice you.
Under my blade, you are mine to control.
Under the blade, there is nowhere you can go.

March 15, 1989

Welcome to the Club

It started with a whisper, which you think I can't hear.
Then comes the giggles whenever I'm near.
You said I was cute, and I wondered why.
When you asked me out, I should have known it was a lie.
The rumors you spread cut me like a knife.
You think this is a joke, but you are ruining my life!
Why did you tell everyone I was gay? I
guess I was the star in your game.
Now I got to live with the shame. You played
your part. You broke my heart.
You and your friends had a good laugh.
I choke on my anger, waiting for the humiliation
to pass. You pressed, and you pressed.
You kicked me when I was on the floor.
Congratulations! I can't take it anymore.
I wish I saw the sign on your door.

*Welcome to the club. You can come right in, just
as long as you have the right color skin.
Welcome to the club. You can have a seat,
just as long as you're not too obese.
What are you doing here? You don't have the right color hair.
Oh my god! I can't believe what I saw.
Was that Adam kissing Steve?
I think we are going to have to ask them to leave.
Welcome to the club. Spreading hate instead of love.*

I want to be accepted. How do I fit in?
I want to be respected. Why can't I find a friend?
Your betrayal started when you said hello.
I thought you were my friend, but I was just a clown in your show.
Everything you said was a lie. How could you look me in the eye?
You swore we were close with every secret I exposed.
I bet you were laughing inside,

While I had tears in my eyes.
I can't take it anymore! Why did you tell
everyone that I was a whore?
I wish I could read the sign on the door.

*Welcome to the club. You can come right in, just
as long as you have the right color skin.
Welcome to the club. You can have a seat,
just as long as you're not too obese.
What are you doing here? You don't have the right color hair.
Oh my god! I can't believe what I saw.
Was that Adam kissing Steve?
I think we are going to have to ask them to leave.
Welcome to the club. Spreading hate instead of love.*

Yes. I am fat. No. I'm not gay.
I can hear everything that you say.
You call me geek. You call me nerd.
You like to hurt people with your words.
They cut to the bone, deeper than any knife.
You don't stop until you take a life.
You like power. You want more.
You hang your sign over your door.

*Welcome to the club. You can come right in, just
as long as you have the right color skin.
Welcome to the club. You can have a seat,
just as long as you're not too obese.
What are you doing here? You don't have the right color hair.
Oh my god! I can't believe what I saw.
Was that Adam kissing Steve?
I think we are going to have to ask them to leave.
Welcome to the club. Spreading hate instead of love.*

July 11, 2019

WILD IN THE STREETS

Just a boy, but forced to be a man. Running
around town without any plan.
Grade A, top of the class. His future was so
bright; now it is all in the past.
He was going to be somebody. How could he fail?
I am sorry, son, but that ship has sailed.
He fell in with the wrong crowd. All they
did was just bring him down.
They left him looking like the class clown.
He had no daddy to set him straight and mommy just got baked.

Running wild in the streets, you think you are so tough.
Wild in the streets until they slap on the cuffs.
Running wild in the streets, living life so fast.
Wild in the streets, you just ran out of gas.

Now he is in a gang, and he has no fear.
He looks around to make sure no one can see his tears.
He thinks no more do I have to be alone.
Maybe, I finally found a home.
He tells himself everything will be all right until that dreadful night.
They gave him a gun and told him to be a man.
He was too nervous. He was too scared.
How could he say no? They would never understand.

Running wild in the streets, you think you are so tough.
Wild in the streets until they slap on the cuffs.
Running wild in the streets, living life so fast.
Wild in the streets, you just ran out of gas.

He just wanted to be noticed by Mom and Dad.
His wish came true. You are a star. You are on the
news, and everyone knows who you are.
He shot that man. He shot him dead. Now you
are left alone. Where are your friends?

He thought that they were cool. Now they do not even know you.
They left you alone to take the rap, and
now your life is in a world of crap.
He got sentenced to life, and now you got to be somebody's wife.
Now you got to spend your life behind bars.
I hope it was worth it, superstar.

Running wild in the streets, you think you are so tough.
Wild in the streets until they slap on the cuffs.
Running wild in the streets, living life so fast.
Wild in the streets, you just ran out of gas.

March 18, 2017

AGAIN

Why have you left me all alone, again?
What have I done that was so wrong, again?
How can I fix it when I don't even know what I did?
Where do we go from here? Are we lovers? Are we friends?

Girl, you got me spinning around, again.
Your love is like a puzzle; where do I begin?
You got me banging my head against the wall.
Your love is a riddle I can't solve.

Why do we have to play these games, again?
Girl, can you tell me when is it gonna end?
Girl, where did our love go, and how did it get so cold?
You say you want to be with me, but you're not at home.

Girl, you got me spinning around, again.
Your love is like a puzzle, where do I begin?
You got me banging my head against the wall.
Your love is a riddle I can't solve.

Why do you cause me so much pain?
How can you say you love me, then you walk away?
What do you hope to gain? You're driving me insane.
Girl, will you take the blame?
When is enough, enough?
This time I called your bluff.
Girl, where you running to, and who's gonna be your fool
Now that we are through?
Girl, you got me spinning around again, and now it's gonna end.

May 11, 2017

About the Author

Michael Jefferson was born in New Bedford, Massachusetts. *Portal* is his second book. His first book, *Sweet Jen*, is a celebration of his late wife, Jennifer. Michael graduated from New Bedford High School in 1989. High school is where he discovered his love for writing and has been writing ever since. He has overcome many obstacles in his life with the help of his son, family, and friends. He is very thankful to them all for giving him the strength and inspiration to keep on writing and to keep on living.

CPSIA information can be obtained
at www.ICGtesting.com
Printed in the USA
BVHW092043290322
632749BV00004B/554